Speaking The Word!

By Robert A. Allen

C.S.S. Publishing Company, Inc.
Lima, Ohio

SPEAKING THE WORD

Copyright © 1991 by
CSS Publishing Company, Inc.
Lima, Ohio

Reprinted 1993, 2002

You may copy the material in this publication if you are the original purchaser, for use as it was intended (worship material for worship use; educational material for classroom use; dramatic material for staging and production). No additional permission is required from the publisher for such copying by the original purchaser only. Inquiries should be addressed to: Permissions, CSS Publishing Company, Inc., P.O. Box 4503, Lima, Ohio 45802-4503.

Scriptures are "from the *HOLY BIBLE, NEW INTERNATIONAL VERSION.* Copyright © 1973, 1978, 1984 International Bible Society. Used by permission of Zondervan Bible Publishers. All rights reserved"; the *King James Version of the Bible,* in the public domain; and from the *New American Standard Bible,* © 1960, 1962, 1963, 1968, 1971, 1972, 1973, 1975, 1977 by The Lockman Foundation. Used by permission.

Library of Congress Cataloging-in-Publication Data

Allen, Robert A., 1946-
    Speaking the Word : scriptures for the speaking choir / Robert A. Allen.
      p.   cm.
    ISBN 1-55673-356-9
    1. Bible—Liturgical lessons, English. 2. Choral recitations.
  I. Title. II. Title: Speaking choir.
    BV199.A2A45   1991
  264'.34—dc20   91-18749
                                                                                      CIP

For more information about CSS Publishing Company resources, visit our website at www.csspub.com or e-mail us at custserv@csspub.com or call (800) 241-4056.

9155 / ISBN 1-55673-356-9   PRINTED IN U.S.A.

Dedicated to the members of the Pillsbury Players, past and present, whose presentation of these Scripture arrangements is exceeded only by their commitment to the Scriptures themselves.

TABLE OF CONTENTS

Foreword   7
Introduction   9
Christmas   15
   Matthew 2:1-12
   Luke 1:26-38
   Luke 1:46-55
   Luke 1:68-79
   Isaiah 9-11, 65

Easter   28
   Matthew 26, 27; John 18
   John 18:39—19:22
   Matthew 28:1-9, Luke 24:1-12
   John 20:1-18

Mother's Day   42
   Proverbs 31:10-31

Father's Day   46
   Judges 13:8, Proverbs 2, 3, 4, 20, 33,
   Ephesians 6

Children   49
   Jeremiah 1, 31, Psalm 139, Mark 9:36, 10:14
   Psalm 127, 128

Heaven   55
   John 14, Revelation 21

Praise   59
   Psalm 24
   Psalm 48, Luke 19
   Psalm 98
   Psalm 115
   Psalm 145

Day of Remembrance   **71**
   Psalm 137

Trust in God   **73**
   Psalm 3

Spiritual Gifts   **75**
   Ephesians 4, Romans 12, 1 Corinthians 12

Prayer   **78**
   Isaiah 65:24, Matthew 7:9-11, Luke 22:39-46

Salvation   **81**
   Romans 5

Money   **84**
   Luke 12:15-21

The Armor of God   **86**
   Ephesians 6:10-17

The Occult   **89**
   Isaiah 8:19-20, Acts 19:13-20,
   1 Chronicles 33

Service   **93**
   Matthew 20:1-16

Missions   **96**
   Matthew 5:13-15, Luke 8:16-18, 11:33-36
   Luke 24:46-48, Acts 1, 8, 13, 14,
   Matthew 28:18-20

FOREWORD

We who have worked with churches and Christian schools in the areas of oral presentation of literature and choral reading, and, who have sat in church and dreaded the responsive reading part of the service because of the mutilation of Scripture that was to follow have waited patiently (not so patiently at times) for a book like *Speaking The Word!*

Scripture reading by a layperson (or anyone who has not practiced the passage) and responsive readings by the congregation usually fall far short of what these segments of the worship service should be and they therefore become a time of general napping for everyone.

Robert A. Allen has successfully and succinctly identified the problem and offers the only attempt I've seen at a solution: the church speaking choir. He has not only provided the reader with guidelines for selecting and training the speaking choir but also has given an excellent range of readings from the Bible that will serve as performances for choral services and as models for the choir director to fashion further readings. He has expertly arranged these readings for maximum impact and even given stage directions for visual and oral effect. Any person interested in using Scripture as an important part of the church service can use this book to accomplish that.

It is obvious to me that a pastor or choir director who grasps the significance of what Robert A. Allen has done here and understands his statements about the importance of Scripture reading in the church service will use the book and practice faithfully what he teaches in *Speaking The Word!*

                    Donald A. Garlock, PhD.
                    Professor of Mass Communications
                    Liberty University

INTRODUCTION

It's Sunday morning and the atmosphere in the church auditorium is charged with a worshipful sense of expectancy. The organist has prepared a prelude based on the theme from "To God Be the Glory." The choir is excited about sharing a new rendition of "Praise Ye the Lord, the Almighty," written expressly for them by a talented young church musician. The pianist has chosen "Majesty" for the offertory, a personal and congregational favorite. The song leader has selected hymns which focus the hearts of the worshipers on exalting God, preparing them for the minister's announced message of the day, "Try Praise!" based on Psalm 145. A soloist has prepared to sing "My Tribute." A small chamber group will play "Thine Be the Glory." A reverent hush settles over the assembly as souls and minds are quieted and centered on worship.

Then, just before the message begins, the time arrives that is described in the order of service as the Responsive Reading. Suddenly, a congregation which has been extremely responsive to the spirit of the meeting becomes totally unresponsive. The reader chosen to lead this portion of the service has not bothered to look through the verses ahead of time. He reads with his head buried in the pages of the text, hurrying through the passage as if there were a trophy waiting for him at the finish line. He bobs his head slightly to signal the beginning of the congregational reading, then shuffles nervously as the people haltingly try to match his furious pace. By the third or fourth "response" most have given up, while the remnant follows the lead of one vigorous voice from the rear.

Is this the condition of the public reading of Scripture in your church? Is it desperately in need of major surgery? Has it already expired and been entombed with other memories of traditions long past?

Perhaps it's not the responsive reading that destroys the worshipful attitude of your assembly. John Wesley said that a certain congregation of his day ought to pay its clergyman for not reading aloud from the Bible. There is many a pastor who spends 20 hours or more preparing a sermon and then exerts no effort at all in preparing to read aloud the passage on which that sermon is based. Yet all would agree with Arthur J. Gossip of Glasgow, Scotland, who said, "Compared to it (Scripture reading) our own poor bits of sermons are a trivial affair, a mere footnote in small print."

Certainly the oral reading of Scripture ought to have a prominent place in the worship of the church. Scripture readings are being used effectively. They are a part of most worship liturgies, as calls to worship, responsive readings, or preparation for the preaching portion of the service. But if Scripture reading is going to assume the prominence in worship that it deserves by its very nature as the Word of God, it must be accorded a place of honor at least equivalent to the other aspects of the worship service. It should be practiced as much as the choir number, prepared as effectively as the sermon, and prayed over as extensively as the invitation. One way to accomplish this is addressed in this book: the organization and training of a speaking choir.

A speaking choir? What's that?

It's Sunday morning and the atmosphere in the church auditorium is charged with a worshipful sense of expectancy. As the organist finishes a thrilling prelude, 10 people move quietly to the platform and turn to face the audience. First in unison, and then by means of solo and ensemble voices, they speak the familiar words of the 145th Psalm, "I will extol thee, my God, O king; and I will bless thy name for ever and ever." As they speak, the significance of the Scripture becomes clear in the minds of the listeners, and they discover, perhaps for the first time, the intent of the psalmist, who was inspired to say, "My mouth will speak in praise of the Lord (Psalm 145:21, NIV)."

Speaking the praise of the Lord is what a speech choir is all about. Young people at Bible camp, children in a Christian school, college students involved in campus productions, and adults in your church get excited when exposed to this opportunity for serving God and sharing his book. "Special numbers" have been restricted to the musical few for too many years. So get a group of people together, practice hard, and "speak in praise of the Lord."

Preparation Of The Speaking Choir

James Black, lecturing at Union Theological Seminary of Virginia in 1924, said of Scripture reading, "It is the hardest thing in the service to do well." Rather than allowing such a statement to discourage a worship leader, it would be better to take it as a challenge to improve. Certainly the material to be shared is supremely worth the effort.

In preparing a group or an individual for the reading of Scripture, remember you are echoing the voice of God. "Hear, O heavens, and give ear, O earth," said the prophet Isaiah to the congregation of Israel, "for the Lord hath spoken." We need to have that same conviction of the importance of the message we proclaim.

Study the passage until you understand the meaning. That will involve more than just knowing how to pronounce all of the words correctly. You are preparing to interpret the passage to an audience through your reading, and that will be impossible if you don't understand it yourself. Research biographical and historical backgrounds. Compare the way passages are rendered in various translations. This will often be a tremendous aid to understanding. Use a concordance, Bible dictionary, or commentaries to learn usages in the original languages of the Bible. Understanding theological implications will contribute greatly to the subsequent ministry of performance.

The key to effectiveness in any ministry of interpretation is communication of meaning. "Your success in getting your listeners to respond to a selection is not likely to exceed your own response to that selection," says the authors of the interpretation text *Communicative Reading* (Bowen, Aggert and Rickert, *Communicative Reading*, Fourth Edition, Macmillan Publishing Co, New York, 1978). Your primary goal for a speaking choir is the clear communication of the gospel message. The way you will reach that goal is by making the best possible use of your voice and body to communicate the message.

There are really only four things you can change about your voice: pacing, volume, pitch and quality. Almost all of our oral communication results from the variations of these four aspects. Certain basic rules apply to each; for example, the interpreter must be certain he or she is projecting, speaking loudly enough to be heard. But the real communication of meaning comes through the capacity of the human voice to vary these four aspects. Variety of volume is more important than being loud or soft. Variations in volume can express excitement, fear, anger, pity, reverence, awe, pride, dominance, and weakness.

The basic rule for pacing is not to rush so that words lose their meaning from being muddled together. But that rule should not be used to justify a lack of variety in pacing. There are passages in Scripture which plead to be read with a rapid pace. Psalm 47:1 "Clap your hands, all you nations; shout to God with cries of joy," would lose all vitality if spoken by a plodder. Chloe Armstrong of Baylor University says, "The oral interpreter should practice reading at different tempos until he has developed a flexible voice, one that can respond and reflect the mood-intensity of the material. A change in tempo can gain the attention of the listeners and can intensify the feeling of the literature" (*Oral Interpretation of Biblical Literature*, Chloe Armstrong, Burgess Publishing, Minneapolis, 1968). Practice until you discover the pacing which underscores the mood of the passage. Every time that mood changes, your pacing should change.

Another facet of pacing that deserves attention by the speaking choir is the pause. Most church audiences are familiar with the Scriptures. So the interpreter must seek for means of emphasis that will focus the attention of the listeners on even the most familiar passage. We must help them hear beyond the words, to the meaning. One of the most effective methods of emphasis available to the oral reader is the pause. A thought-filled silence will enable listeners to reflect on what has just been said. It can also cause them to anticipate and focus their attention on what is to come. The thoughtful pause is the idea behind the familiar "selah" of the psalmist, which means "think about that." Apparently the writers of the psalms didn't trust their audience to use thoughtful silences, so they gave verbal instructions. Since the nature of audiences has not changed since Old Testament times, communicators today may also find themselves using other means such as facial expression and movement to augment the pause.

The ability of the human voice to speak at a variety of pitch levels is probably the most effective way of communicating exact meanings. You can take a one syllable word like "so" and make it take on a variety of meanings simply by varying the pitch, inflection, or intonation of that syllable. It could mean anything from "I've caught you at last" to "It's all over." Changing the pitch of one word at the end of a sentence can mean the difference between a statement of fact and a question.

It is possible with practice to greatly increase the variety of pitch levels at which a person speaks, thus increasing the expressiveness of the voice. Your goal should not be to produce a performance at which people will marvel over your range and ability. The purpose of expanding the range should be to increase your success in conveying the exact meaning of the passage. A monotonous voice cannot convey as many meanings as an expressive voice.

Another facet of pitch which is extremely important for the speaking choir is optimum pitch. Optimum pitch is the range of the voice where an individual is able to speak most comfortably. It corresponds loosely to whether a singer is a soprano, alto, tenor or bass. In choral speaking the variety of pitch in voices is usually spoken of in terms of dark and light. Those voices with a lower pitch are termed dark voices and those with a higher pitch are called light voices. Tenors and sopranos would normally have light speaking voices while altos and basses would have dark speaking voices. The selections for the speaking choir are arranged in terms of light and dark voices. During practice you will want to try different combinations of voices to determine which ones blend well for the best effect.

Vocal quality is the aspect of communication which often receives the least consideration because of the mistaken notion that nothing can be done about the way a person sounds. The fact that you do not sound the same when you have a sinus condition should convince you that a change in vocal quality is possible. In fact, changes in basic quality of the voice are common. Quality changes unconsciously depending on our emotional state. As interpreters we need to learn to control vocal quality. The key is to be intellectually and emotionally stimulated by the selection. As body tensions adjust to the meaning being expressed, the appropriate expressive quality will result.

Although memorization is not necessary for the speaking choir, rehearse each selection until you can perform without the script. That way you will be completely confident that you are doing the best possible job for the glory of God.

Christmas

Matthew 2:1-12 (NIV)

Dark Solo One:	Magi,
Dark Solo Two:	magi,
Dark Solo Three:	magi
Dark Trio:	from the East
All Dark:	came to Jerusalem.
Dark Solo One:	Magi
Dark Trio:	from the East,
Dark Duet:	the time of King Herod,
Dark Solo Two:	magi
Dark Trio:	from the East
Light Solo One:	after Jesus was born in Bethlehem.
Dark Trio:	Where is the one who has been born king of the Jews?
Light Solo Two:	*[Quickly, as if repeating gossip.]* King of the Jews?
Light Solo Three:	King of the Jews?
Light Duet:	King of the Jews?
Dark Solo Three:	We have seen his star
Dark Trio:	in the East
Dark Solo Three:	and have come to worship him.
All Light:	When King Herod heard this,
Dark Solo Four:	he was troubled,
All:	and all Jerusalem with him.
All Light:	When he had called together all the people's chief priests and

	teachers of the law, he asked them
Dark Solo Four:	where the Christ was to be born.
All Dark:	In Bethlehem of Judea, for this is what the prophet has written:
Light/Dark Duet:	But you,
Light Solo:	Bethlehem,
Light/Dark Duet:	in the land of Judah, are by no means the least among the rulers of Judah,
Light/Dark Quartet:	for out of you will come a ruler,
All:	a ruler
Light/Dark Quartet:	who will be the shepherd of my people Israel.
Dark Solo Four:	Then Herod called the magi
Light Solo One:	secretly,
Dark Solo Four:	secretly,
Light Solo Two:	secretly,
Light Solo Three:	secretly,
Dark Solo Four:	and found out from them
Dark Trio:	the exact time the star had appeared.
All Light:	He sent them to
Light Solo One:	Bethlehem
All Light:	and said,
Dark Solo Four:	Go and make a careful search for the child. As soon as you find him, report to me, so that I, too, may go and worship him.
Light Solo Three:	I, too? May go and worship him?
Dark Solo Four:	I, too, may go and worship him!

All Light:	After they had heard the king,
Dark Trio:	they went their way.
Dark Solo One:	And the star
Dark Solo Two:	which they had seen in the east
Dark Solo Three:	went ahead of them
Dark Trio:	until it stopped
Light Duet:	over the place where the child was.
All Light:	When they saw the star,
Dark Trio:	they were overjoyed.
Light Duet:	On coming to the house, they saw the child
Light Solo One:	with his mother, Mary,
Dark Trio:	and they bowed down and worshiped him.
All Dark:	Then they opened their treasures and presented him with gifts:
Dark Solo One:	gold,
Dark Solo Two:	incense,
Dark Solo Three:	myrrh.
All:	And having been warned
All Light:	in a dream
All:	not to go back to Herod —
Dark Solo Four:	Not to go back to Herod?
Dark Trio:	They returned to their country by another route.
Dark Solo One:	Magi,
Dark Solo Two:	magi,
Dark Solo Three:	magi,
All:	from the East!

Christmas

Luke 1:26-38 (NASB)

All Dark:	Now in the sixth month the angel Gabriel was sent from God
All Light:	to a city in Galilee, called Nazareth,
Light Trio:	to a virgin
Dark Trio	engaged to a man whose name was Joseph,
All Dark:	of the descendants of David;
All Light:	and the virgin's name was
Light Solo:	Mary.
All Dark:	And coming in, he said to her,
Dark Solo:	Hail, favored one! The Lord is with you.
Light Trio:	But she was greatly troubled at this statement
Light Solo:	and kept pondering what kind of salutation this might be.
All Dark:	And the angel said unto her,
Dark Solo:	Do not be afraid, Mary;
Add All Light:	for you have found favor with God.
Dark Solo:	And behold, you will conceive in your womb
Add All Light:	and bear a son
Dark Solo:	and you shall call his name
Light Solo:	Jesus,
Light Solo Two:	Jesus,
Light Duet:	Jesus.

Dark Solo:	And you shall call his name
All:	JESUS.
All Dark:	He shall be great.
All Light:	He will be called the Son of the Most High.
Dark Solo:	The Lord God will give him
All Dark:	the throne of his father David.
Dark Solo:	And he will reign over the house of Jacob.
All Light	And his kingdom will have no end.
All:	His kingdom will have no end.
Light Trio:	And Mary said to the angel,
Light Solo:	How can this be, since I am a virgin?
Dark Solo:	The Holy Spirit will come upon you,
Add Light Trio:	and the power of the Most High will overshadow you
Add All Light:	and for that reason the holy offspring shall be called
All:	the Son of God.
Dark Solo:	And behold, even your relative Elizabeth has also conceived a son in her old age:
Add All Light:	she who was called barren is now in her sixth month,
Dark Solo:	for nothing will be impossible with God.
All Light:	Nothing will be impossible with God.
Light Solo:	Nothing will be impossible with God.

Christmas

Luke 1:46:55 (KJV)

A Scripture Chorus For Women

All:	My soul doth magnify the Lord.
Light Solo:	My soul doth magnify the Lord.
Light Solo Two:	And my spirit hath rejoiced in God my Savior,
Light Duet:	rejoiced in God my Savior,
Light Trio:	rejoiced in God my Savior.
Light Solo:	For he hath regarded the low estate of his handmaiden.
Light Solo Two:	From henceforth all generations shall call me blessed.
All Dark:	Blessed art thou among women
All Light:	and blessed is the fruit of thy womb.
All:	Blessed art thou among women.
Light Duet:	For he that is mighty hath done to me great things,
All:	and holy,
Light Solo Three:	holy,
Dark Solo:	HOLY
All:	is his name.
Light Solo:	And his mercy is on them
Light Duet:	that fear him,
All Light:	from generation
All Dark:	to generation.

Dark Solo:	He hath shewed strength with his arm.
Light Solo Three:	He hath scattered the proud in the imagination of their hearts.
Dark Solo Two:	He hath put down the mighty from their seats
Light Solo Four:	and exalted them of low degree.
Dark Solo Three:	He hath filled the hungry with good things,
Light Solo Five:	and the rich he hath sent empty away.
All Light:	He hath helped his servant Israel,
All Dark:	in remembrance of his mercy:
All:	As he spake to our fathers,
Dark Solo:	to Abraham,
All:	and to his seed for ever.
Dark Solo Two:	For ever?
All:	To his seed for ever.
Light Solo:	My soul doth magnify the Lord.

Christmas

Luke 1:68-79 (KJV)

A Scripture Chorus For Men

Dark Solo:	Blessed be the Lord God of Israel.
All:	Blessed be the Lord God of Israel.
Dark Solo:	For he hath visited,
All Dark:	visited and redeemed his people,
Dark Solo:	and hath raised up a horn of salvation,
All Light:	a horn of salvation for us
All:	in the house of his servant David,
All Light:	as he spake by the mouth of his holy prophets
Light Solo:	that we should be saved from our enemies —
Dark Solo:	a thousand shall fall at thy side and ten thousand at thy right hand; but it shall not come nigh thee —
Light Solo Two:	and from the hand of all that hate us;
Dark Solo Two:	The Lord shall cause thine enemies that rise up against thee to be smitten before thy face:

Light Solo Three:	to perform the mercy promised to our holy fathers,
Dark Solo Three:	The eternal God is thy refuge, and underneath are the everlasting arms.
Light Solo Four:	Remember his holy covenant,
All Light:	the oath which he sware to our father Abraham.
All Dark:	In thy seed shall all the nations of the earth be blessed; because thou hast obeyed my voice.
Dark Solo:	Grant unto us, that we, being delivered out of the hand of our enemies,
Dark Duet:	might serve him without fear,
Dark Trio:	in holiness
Dark Quartet:	and righteousness
All Dark:	all the days of our life.
All:	Blessed be the Lord God of Israel,
Dark Solo:	for he hath visited,
All Dark:	visited and redeemed his people.
Light Solo:	And thou, child, shalt be called
All Light:	the prophet of the Highest,
All Dark:	the prophet of the Highest,
All:	the prophet of the Highest:
Light Solo:	For thou shalt go before the face of the Lord
Light Duet:	to prepare his ways,
Light Trio:	to give knowledge of salvation unto his people

Light Quartet:	by the remission of their sins
All Light:	through the tender mercy of our God,
All:	whereby the Dayspring from on High —
Dark Solo:	before the face of the Lord —
All:	the Dayspring from on High —
Light Solo:	before the face of the Lord —
All:	the Dayspring from on High hath visited
Dark Solo:	us,
Light Solo:	us,
Dark Solo Two:	us,
Light Solo Two:	us,
All Light:	us —
Light Solo:	the Dayspring from on High —
Light Solo Three:	*[softly]* to give light to them that sit in darkness —
Light Solo:	the Dayspring from on High —
Dark Solo Three:	and in the shadow of death —
Light Solo:	the Dayspring from on High —
All Light:	to guide our feet into the way of peace —
All Dark:	THE LORD.
Light Solo:	Blessed be the Lord God of Israel.

Christmas
Isaiah 9-11, 65 (KJV)

The Prince of Peace

All Dark	His name shall be called
All:	The Prince of Peace,
Light Solo:	for unto us a child is born,
Light Solo Two:	unto us a son is given:
Dark Solo:	the government shall be upon his shoulder:
All Dark:	and his name shall be called
Light Solo:	Wonderful,
Dark Solo Two:	Counselor,
Light Solo Two:	the Mighty God,
Dark Solo Three:	the Everlasting Father,
All:	the Prince of Peace.
Light Trio:	The spirit of the Lord shall rest upon him,
Light Solo:	the spirit of wisdom and understanding,
Light Solo Two:	the spirit of counsel and might,
Light Solo Three:	the spirit of knowledge and of the fear of the Lord;
Light Trio:	and shall make him of quick understanding in the fear of the Lord:
Dark Solo:	and he shall not judge after the sight of his eyes,
Dark Solo Two:	neither reprove after the hearing of his ears:

Dark Solo Three:	but with righteousness shall he judge the poor,
Dark Solo Four:	and reprove with equity for the meek of the earth:
Dark Duet:	and he shall smite the earth with the rod of his mouth,
Dark Quartet:	and with the breath of his lips shall he slay the wicked.
All Light:	And righteousness shall be the girdle of his loins,
All Dark:	and faithfulness the girdle of his reins.
Light Solo:	The wolf also
Add Light Duet:	shall dwell with the lamb,
Dark Solo:	and the leopard
Add Dark Duet:	shall lie down with the kid;
Light Solo Two:	and the calf
Dark Solo Two:	and the young lion
Light Solo Three:	and the fatling
Light/Dark Trio:	together;
Light/Dark Quartet:	and a little child shall lead them.
Light Solo:	And the sucking child
Dark Solo:	shall play on the hole of the asp,
Light Solo Two:	and the weaned child
Dark Solo Two:	shall put his hand on the cockatrice's den.
All Light:	They shall not hurt nor destroy in all my holy mountain:
All Dark:	in all my holy mountain:
All:	for the earth shall be full of the knowledge of the Lord,
All Dark:	as the waters cover the sea,
All Light:	as the waters cover the sea,
All:	as the waters cover the sea.

Light Trio:	Praise the Lord.
Light Quartet:	Call upon his name.
Light Duet:	Declare his doings among the people,
Dark Duet:	make mention that his name is exalted.
All:	His name is exalted.
Light Solo:	Sing,
Light Solo Two:	sing,
Light Solo Three:	sing,
Light Solo Four:	sing,
Light Quintet:	sing unto the Lord;
Dark Quartet:	for he hath done excellent things:
Light Quintet:	Cry out and shout,
Dark Quartet:	cry out and shout,
All:	cry out and shout,
Dark Solo:	for great is the Holy One of Israel in the midst of thee.
All Dark:	His name shall be called
All Light:	the Prince,
All Dark:	the Prince
All:	of Peace.

The Crucifixion

Matthew 26-27, John 18 (KJV)

From The Viewpoint Of The Apostle Peter

All:	Then saith Jesus unto them,
Dark/Light Duet:	All ye shall be offended because of me this night.
All Light:	Peter answered and said unto him,
Dark Quartet:	Though all men shall be offended because of thee,
Dark Solo:	yet will I never,
Dark Solo Two:	never,
Dark Solo Three:	never,
Dark Solo Four:	never,
Dark Quartet:	never be offended.
Dark/Light Duet:	Verily I say unto thee that this night before the cock crow thou shalt deny me thrice.
Dark Quartet:	Though I should die with thee,
Dark Duet:	die with thee,
Dark Duet Two:	die with thee,
Dark Quartet:	yet will I not deny thee.
All:	Likewise also said all the disciples.
Light Solo:	Then cometh Jesus unto a place called Gethsemane
Light Duet:	and saith unto the disciples,
Dark/Light Duet:	sit ye here, while I go and pray yonder.

Light Duet:	And he cometh unto the disciples and findeth them asleep
Light Solo:	and said unto Peter,
Dark/Light Duet:	What, could ye not watch with me one hour?
All:	Then came they and laid hands on Jesus and took him.
All Dark:	Simon Peter, having a sword, drew it,
Dark Solo:	and smote the high priest's servant
Dark Duet:	and cut off his right ear.
Dark/Light Duet:	Put up thy sword into the sheath; the cup which my Father hath given me, shall I not drink it?
Light Trio:	Then the band and the captain and officers of the Jews took Jesus
All Light:	and bound him
All:	and led him away.
Dark Quartet:	But Peter followed him
Dark Solo:	afar off.
Light Trio:	Then saith the damsel that kept the door unto Peter,
Light Solo:	Art not thou also one of this man's disciples?
Dark Quartet:	I am not.
Dark Duet:	*[Echo]* I am not.
Dark Solo:	*[Echo]* I am not.
Light Trio:	And the servants
Dark Trio:	and officers stood there,
Light/Dark Trio:	and they warmed themsevles.

Dark Quartet:	And Peter stood with them, and warmed himself.
Light/Dark Trio:	Art not thou also one of his disciples?
Dark Quartet:	I am not.
Dark Duet:	*[Echo]* I am not.
Dark Solo:	*[Echo]* I am not.
Light/Dark Trio:	One of the servants of the high priest,
Light Solo:	being his kinsman whose ear Peter cut off, saith,
Dark Solo Two:	Did not I see thee in the garden with him?
Light/Dark Trio:	Thy speech betrayeth thee.
Dark Quartet:	Then began he
Dark Duet:	to curse
Dark Duet Two:	and to swear,
Dark Quartet:	I know not the man,
Dark Trio:	*[Louder]* know not the man,
Dark Duet:	*[Louder]* not the man,
Dark Solo:	*[Simultaneously]* the man.
All Light:	*[Simultaneously]* And immediately
Light Trio:	the cock crew,
Light Duet:	*[Echo]* the cock crew,
Light Solo:	*[Echo]* the cock crew.
Dark Quartet:	And Peter went out
Dark Duet:	and wept
Dark Solo:	bitterly.

The Crucifixion
John 18:39-19:22 (KJV)

Dark Solo:	Will ye therefore that I release unto you the King of the Jews?
All:	Not this man, but Barabbas.
Dark Solo:	Then Pilate therefore took Jesus and scourged him.
Dark Duet:	And the soldiers platted a crown of thorns and put it on his head,
Dark Trio:	and they put on him a purple robe and said,
All Dark:	Hail, King of the Jews! Hail, King of the Jews!
Dark Trio:	And they smote him with their hands.
Dark Solo:	Behold, I bring him forth to you, that ye may know that I find no fault in him.
Light Solo:	Then came Jesus forth,
Light Duet:	wearing the crown of thorns
Light Trio:	and the purple robe.
Dark Solo:	Behold, the man!
Dark Duet:	When the chief priests therefore and officers saw him, they cried out, saying,
All Dark:	Crucify him, crucify him.
Dark Solo:	Take ye him and crucify him: for I find no fault in him.

Dark Solo Two:	No fault in him?
Dark Solo:	I find no fault in him.
Dark Solo Three:	No fault in him?
Dark Solo:	I find . . .
Dark Trio:	*[Interrupting]* We have a law,
Dark Solo Two:	and by our law
Dark Trio:	he ought to die,
Dark Solo Three:	because he made himself the Son of God,
Light Solo:	*[Whispered]* the Son of God,
Light Solo Two:	*[Whispered]* the Son of God,
Light Solo Three:	*[Whispered]* the Son of God,
Light Trio:	the Son of God.
All Light:	When Pilate therefore heard that saying, he was the more afraid
All Dark:	and went again into the judgment hall and saith unto Jesus,
Dark Solo:	Whence art thou? *[Pause]* Whence art thou?
Light Solo:	But Jesus gave him no answer.
Dark Solo:	Speakest thou not unto me? Knowest thou not that I have power to crucify thee and have power to release thee?
Dark/Light Duet:	Thou couldst have no power at all against me, except it were given thee from above: therefore he that delivered me unto thee hath the greater sin.
Dark Trio:	He that delivered me? *[Pause]* The greater sin?
Light Duet:	From henceforth Pilate sought to release him:

All Light:	but the Jews cried out, saying,
Dark Duet:	If thou let this man go, thou art not Caesar's friend:
Second Dark Duet:	whosoever maketh himself a king speaketh against Caesar,
Dark Duet:	not Caesar's friend,
Second Dark Duet:	speaketh against Caesar.
Light Trio:	When Pilate therefore heard that saying,
Light Quartet:	he brought Jesus forth, and sat down in the judgment seat.
All Light:	And about the sixth hour, he saith unto the Jews,
Dark Solo:	Behold your King!

[The next four lines are said simultaneously.]

Dark Trio:	Crucify him.
Light Trio:	Away with him.
Second Dark Trio:	Away with him.
Second Light Trio:	Crucify him.
Dark Solo:	Shall I crucify your king?
All Dark:	We have no king but Caesar.
All:	No king but Caesar.
All Light:	No king
All Dark:	but Caesar.
Dark Solo:	Then delivered he him therefore unto them to be crucified.
Light Trio:	And they took Jesus and led him away.
Dark/Light Duet:	And he, bearing his cross,
Light Trio:	went forth
Dark/Light Duet:	into a place called
Dark Duet:	the place of a skull,
Light Duet:	*[Echo]* a skull,
Light Solo:	*[Echo]* a skull,

Dark Solo: where they crucified him,
Dark Duet: and two other with him,
Dark Solo Two: on either side
Dark Solo Three: one
Light Trio: and Jesus in the midst.
Dark Solo: And Pilate wrote a title and put it on the cross.
All: Jesus of Nazareth, the King of the Jews?
Dark Solo: The King of the Jews!
Dark Duet: Write not, the King of the Jews:
Second Dark Duet: but that he said, I am the King of the Jews.
Dark Solo: What I have written, I have written.
All: *[In dismay]* The King of the Jews?

The Resurrection

Matthew 28:1-9, Luke 24:1-12, John 20:9-16 (NASB)

All Light:	On the first day of the week
Light Solo:	at early dawn
All Light:	they came to the tomb,
Light Solo:	Mary Magdalene
Light Solo Two:	and the other Mary.
All Dark:	And behold, a severe earthquake had occurred,
Dark Solo:	for an angel of the Lord descended from heaven
Dark Solo Two:	and came and rolled away the stone
Dark Duet:	and sat upon it.
All Dark:	And his appearance was like lightning,
All Light:	and his garment as white as snow;
All:	and the guards shook for fear of him
Dark Quartet:	and became like dead men.
Light Duet:	And as the women were terrified and bowed their faces to the ground, the men said to them,
Dark Duet:	Why do ye seek the Living One among the dead?
Dark Trio:	He is not here,
Dark Quartet:	but he is risen.

Light Duet:	Has risen?
Light Trio:	He has risen.
All Light:	He has risen.
All:	He has risen!
Dark Duet:	Remember how he spoke to you while he was still in Galilee,
Dark Solo:	saying that the Son of Man must be delivered into the hands of sinful men
Dark Solo Two:	and be crucifed
Dark Duet:	and the third day rise again.
All Light:	And they remembered his words,
Dark Duet:	Go quickly and tell his disciples that he has risen from the dead.
All Light:	He has risen from the dead;
All Dark:	he has risen from the dead;
All:	he has risen from the dead;
Dark Duet:	Behold, he is going before you into Galilee, there you will see him;
All Dark:	you will see him;
All Light:	will see him;
Light Trio:	And they departed quickly from the tomb
Light Solo:	with fear
Light Solo Two:	and great joy
Light Trio:	and ran to report it to his disciples.
All Dark:	And these words appeared to them as nonsense,
Light Solo:	He is risen!
Dark Solo:	Nonsense!

Light Solo Two:	You will see him!
Dark Solo Two:	Nonsense!
All Dark:	And they would not believe them.
All Light:	For as yet they did not understand the Scripture, that he must rise again from the dead.
Light Solo:	But Mary was standing outside the tomb, weeping;
Light Duet:	and so, as she wept, she stooped and looked into the tomb;
All Light:	and she beheld two angels in white, sitting,
Dark Solo:	one at the head
Dark Solo Two:	and one at the feet,
All Light:	where the body of Jesus had been lying.
Dark Duet:	Woman, why are you weeping?
Light Solo:	Because they have taken away my Lord, and I do not know where they have laid him.
Light Trio:	When she had said this, she turned around
All Light:	and beheld Jesus standing there
Light Trio:	and did not know that it was Jesus.
Dark/Light Duet:	Woman, why are you weeping? Whom are you seeking?
Light Trio:	Supposing him to be the gardener, she said to him,

Light Solo:	Sir, if you have carried him away, tell me where you have laid him, and I will take him away.
Dark/Light Duet:	Mary.
Light Solo:	Mary?
All Light:	Mary.
Light Solo:	Rabboni!
All Light:	Rabboni! He is risen!
All:	He is risen, indeed!

Easter

John 20:1-18 (NIV)

Light Solo One:	They have taken the Lord out of the tomb,
Dark Solo One:	they have taken the Lord out of the tomb,
Dark/Light Trio:	they have taken the Lord out of the tomb.
All Light:	Early on the first day of the week, while it was still dark, Mary Magdalene went to the tomb
All Dark:	and saw that the stone had been removed from the entrance.
Dark Solo One:	So she came running to Simon Peter
Dark Solo Two:	and the other disciple, the one Jesus loved.
Light Solo One:	They have taken the Lord out of the tomb,
All Light:	and we don't know where they have put him!
Dark Duet:	So Peter and the other disciple started for the tomb. Both were running,
Dark Solo Two:	but the other disciple outran Peter and reached the tomb first.

All Dark:	He bent over and looked in at the strips of linen lying there
Dark Solo Two:	but did not go in.
Dark Solo One:	Then Simon Peter arrived and went into the tomb.
All:	He saw
Light Solo Two:	the strips of linen lying there,
Light Duet:	the burial cloth that had been around Jesus' head.
Light Trio:	The cloth was folded up by itself,
Light Solo Two:	separate from the linen.
Dark Solo Two:	Finally the other disciple, who had reached the tomb first, also went inside.
All:	He saw
Dark Solo Two:	and believed.
All:	They still did not understand from Scripture that Jesus had to rise from the dead.
All Light:	They still did not understand.
Dark Duet:	Then the disciples went back to their homes,
All Light:	did not understand,
Light Solo One:	but Mary stood outside the tomb, crying.
All Light:	Not understand.
Light Solo One:	As she wept, she bent over to look into the tomb
Light/Dark Quartet:	and saw two angels in white, seated where Jesus' body had been,
Light Solo Two:	one at the head
Light Solo Three:	and the other at the foot.

Light Duet:	Woman, why are you crying?
Light Solo One:	They have taken my Lord away,
Light/Dark Quartet:	they have taken my Lord away,
Light Solo One:	and I don't know where they have put him.
All Light:	At this, she turned around and saw Jesus standing there,
Light Solo One:	But she did not realize that it was Jesus.
All Dark:	Woman, why are you crying? Who is it you are looking for?
Light Solo One:	Sir,
Light Trio:	thinking he was the gardener,
Light Solo One:	Sir, if you have carried him away,
All Light:	tell me where you have put him,
Light Solo One:	and I will get him.
All Dark:	Mary.
(A long pause)	
Light Solo One:	Rabboni! Teacher! I have seen the Lord!
Light Duet:	I have seen the Lord!
Light Trio:	I have seen the Lord!
All Light:	I have seen the Lord!
All:	I have seen the Lord!

Mother's Day

Proverbs 31:10-31 (NASB)

**A Scripture Chorus
For Fathers And Children**

All:	An excellent wife, who can find? For her worth is far above jewels.
All Dark:	The heart of her husband trusts in her,
Dark Duet:	and he will have no lack of gain.
Dark Trio:	She does him good
All Light:	and not evil
Dark Trio:	all the days of her life.
Dark Solo:	She looks for wool and flax and works with her hands in delight.
Light Trio:	And his mother would make him a little robe and bring it to him from year to year.
Dark Duet:	She is like merchant ships; she brings her food from afar.
Light Trio:	Then Abigail hurried and took
Light Solo:	two hundred loaves of bread and two jugs of wine
Light Solo Two:	and five sheep already prepared and five measures of roasted grain
Light Solo Three:	and a hundred clusters of raisins and two hunded cakes of figs

Light Trio:	and loaded them on donkeys.
Dark Trio:	She rises also while it is still night and gives food to her household and portions to her maidens.
Light Trio:	So Abraham hurried into the tent to Sarah and said,
All Light:	Quickly, prepare three measures of fine flour, knead it, and make bread cakes.
Dark Quartet:	She considers a field and buys it; from her earnings she plants a vineyard.
Light Trio:	Then Boaz said, On the day you buy the field from the hand of Naomi, you must also acquire Ruth the Moabitess.
Dark Quintet:	She girds herself with strength, and makes her arms strong.
Light Trio:	Then Barak said to her,
Dark Solo:	If you will go with me, then I will go.
Light Solo:	I will surely go with you; nevertheless, the honor shall not be yours on the journey that you are about to take.
All Light:	For the Lord will sell Sisera into the hands of a woman.
Dark Sextet:	She stretches out her hands to the distaff, and her hands grasp the spindle.
All Light:	And all the skilled women spun with their hands and brought

	what they had spun in blue and purple and scarlet material and in fine linen.
Dark Septet:	She extends her hands to the poor; and she stretches out her hands to the needy.
Light Trio:	And when he had come, they brought him into an upper room; and all the widows stood beside him weeping and showing all the tunics and garments that Dorcas used to make while she was with them.
Dark Octet:	She is not afraid of the snow for her household.
Dark Duet:	for all her household are clothed with scarlet.
Light Duet:	She makes coverings for herself; her clothing is fine linen and purple.
All Dark:	Her husband is known in the gates
Dark Solo:	when he sitteth among the elders of the land.
All Light:	She makes linen garments and sells them and supplies belts to the tradesmen.
Dark Trio:	And a certain woman named Lydia, from the city of Thyatira, a seller of purple fabrics, a worshiper of God, was listening.
All Light:	Strength and dignity are her clothing
Light Solo:	and she smiles at the future.

Light Solo Two:	She opens her mouth in wisdom,
Light Solo Three:	and the teachings of kindness is on her tongue.
Dark Solo:	She looks well to the ways of her household
Dark Solo Two:	and does not eat the bread of idleness.
All Children:	Her children rise up and bless her;
All Fathers:	her husband also, and he praises her, saying:
Dark Trio:	Many daughters have done nobly,
All Dark:	but you excel them all.
All:	Charm is deceitful, and beauty is vain, but a woman who fears the Lord, she shall be praised.
All Fathers:	She shall be praised.
All Children:	She shall be praised.
All:	She shall be praised.

Father's Day

Judges 13:8; Proverbs 4, 20, 23; Galatians 4:6-7; Ephesians 6:4 (KJV)

All Dark:	Hear, ye children, the instruction of a father,
Dark Solo:	the instruction of a father,
Dark Solo Two:	a father,
Dark Solo Three:	a father,
Dark Solo Four:	a father,
Dark Solo Five:	a father,
All Dark:	and attend to know understanding.
Dark Trio:	For I was my father's son,
All Dark:	my father's son,
Dark Solo:	tender
Dark Solo Two:	and only beloved
Dark Trio:	in the sight of my mother.
All Dark:	He taught me also, and said unto me,
Dark Solo Three:	Let thine heart retain my words:
Dark Solo Four:	keep my commandments,
All Dark:	and live.
Dark Solo:	Then Manoah entreated the Lord, and said,
Dark Duet:	O my Lord, let the man of God which thou didst send come again,
All Dark:	come again
Dark Duet:	and teach us,

All Dark:	teach us
Dark Duet:	what we shall do unto the child,
All Dark:	what we shall do unto the child that shall be born.
Dark Duet:	How shall we order the child?
All Dark:	How shall we do unto him?
Dark Solo:	Ye fathers, provoke not your children to wrath:
Dark Trio:	but bring them up,
All Dark:	bring them up
Dark Solo Two:	in the nurture
Dark Solo Three:	and admonition
Dark Trio:	of the Lord.
All Dark:	Bring them up
Dark Solo Two:	nurture,
Dark Solo Three:	admonition
All Dark:	of the Lord.
Dark Solo:	The father of the righteous
Dark Trio:	shall greatly rejoice:
All Dark:	greatly rejoice:
Dark Quartet:	and he that begetteth a wise child,
Dark Solo Four:	a wise child
All Dark:	shall have joy of him.
Dark Duet:	Thy father and thy mother shall be glad,
Dark Trio:	and she that bare thee shall rejoice,
Dark Solo:	shall rejoice,
All Dark:	shall rejoice.
Dark Trio:	My son,
Dark Solo:	give me thine heart,
All Dark:	give me thine heart,
Dark Duet:	and let thine eyes observe my ways.

Dark Solo Two:	The just man walketh in his integrity:
Dark Trio:	his children are blessed after him.
All Dark:	I will be a father unto you,
Dark Trio:	and ye shall be my sons and daughters,
All Dark:	saith the Lord Almighty.
Dark Solo:	And because ye are sons,
Dark Quartet:	God hath sent forth the Spirit of his Son into your hearts, crying,
All Dark:	Abba, Father!
Dark Trio:	Abba, Father!
All Dark:	Abba, Father!
Dark Solo:	Wherefore, thou art no more a servant,
Dark Duet:	but a son;
Dark Trio:	and if a son, then an heir of God
All Dark:	through Christ.
Dark Solo:	Abba,
All Dark:	Abba, Father!

Children

Jeremiah 1, 31; Psalm 139; Mark 9:36, 10:14, 16 (KJV)

All:	Thus saith the Lord;
Light Solo:	A voice
Light Trio:	was heard in Ramah,
Light Solo:	A voice was heard in
Light Trio:	lamentation,
Light Solo:	A voice was heard in
Light Trio:	bitter weeping.
All Light:	Rachel,
Light Solo:	weeping,
Light Trio:	weeping for her children, for her children
Light Duet:	*[Echo]* her children,
Light Solo:	*[Echo]* children,
All Light:	Rachel,
Light Solo:	weeping,
All Light:	refused to be comforted for her children,
Light Duet:	*[Echo]* her children,
Light Solo:	*[Echo]* children,
Light Solo Two:	*[Echo]* children,
All:	because they were not.
All Dark:	Suffer the little children to come unto me, and forbid them not: for of such is the kingdom of God.
Light Trio:	Thou hast covered me in my mother's womb.

All:	I will praise thee;
Light Duet:	For I am fearfully
Dark Duet:	and wonderfully made:
Light/Dark Quartet:	marvellous are thy works;
Dark Solo:	and that my soul knoweth right well.
Light Solo:	My substance was not hid from thee
Light Solo Two:	when I was made in secret
Light Solo Three:	and curiously wrought in the lowest parts of the earth.
Dark Solo:	Thine eyes did see my substance,
Dark/Light Duet:	yet being unperfect;
Dark/Light Trio:	and in thy book
Dark/Light Quartet:	all my members were written, which in continuance were fashioned,
Light Solo:	when as yet there was none of them.
All Dark:	In thy book all my members were written,
All Light:	in thy book all my members were written
All:	when as yet there was none of them.
All Dark:	How precious also are thy thoughts unto me, O God!
All Light:	How precious also are thy thoughts unto me.
Dark Duet:	Before I formed thee in the belly, I knew thee;
Dark Quartet:	Before thou camest forth out of the womb, I sanctified thee,

All Dark:	and I ordained thee a prophet unto the nations
All:	before thou camest forth out of the womb.
Light Solo:	And he took a child
Light Duet:	and set him in the midst of them,
Light Trio:	and when he had taken him in his arms, he said unto them,
Dark Quartet:	Whosoever shall receive one of such children in my name,
Dark Solo:	receiveth me:
Light Trio:	And he took them up in his arms,
Light Duet:	put his hands upon them,
Light Solo:	and blessed them.
All Light:	Suffer the little children to come unto me,
All Dark:	Rachel weeping for her children,
All:	for they were not.
Light Solo:	Suffer the little children.

Children

Psalm 127, 128 (NASB)

All Dark:	Unless the Lord builds the house,
All Light:	unless the Lord builds the house,
All Dark:	they labor in vain
All Light:	they labor in vain
All:	they labor in vain who build it;
All Dark:	Unless the Lord guards the city,
Dark Solo:	the watchman keeps awake
All Light:	in vain.
Light Solo:	It is vain for you to rise up early,
Light Solo Two:	to retire late,
Light Solo Three:	to eat the bread of painful labors;
All Light:	for he gives to his beloved,
All Dark:	he gives to his beloved,
Dark Solo:	even in his sleep.
All:	Behold,
All Light:	children,
All Dark:	children,
All Light:	children are a gift,
All Dark:	a gift of the Lord;
All:	children are a gift of the Lord;
Light Solo:	a gift,
Dark Solo:	a gift
All:	of the Lord;
All Light:	The fruit of the womb

All Dark:	is a reward.
Dark Solo:	Like arrows,
Dark Solo Two:	arrows in the hand
Dark Duet:	of a warrior,
Dark Quartet:	so are the children of one's youth.
All Dark:	How blessed is the man whose quiver is full of them,
All Light:	whose quiver is full of them; They shall not be ashamed
All Dark:	when they speak with their enemies in the gate.
Light Solo:	How blessed is everyone who fears the Lord,
Light Duet:	who walks in his ways.
Light/Dark Duet:	When you shall eat of the fruit of your hands,
Light/Dark Quartet:	you will be happy,
Dark Duet:	and it will be well with you.
All Light:	Your wife shall be like a fruitful vine within your house;
Light/Dark Duet:	your children,
Light/Dark Quartet:	your children,
All:	your children like olive plants
All Light:	around your table.
All:	Behold,
Dark Quartet:	for thus shall the man be blessed
All:	who fears the Lord.
All Dark:	The Lord bless you from Zion,
All Light:	the Lord bless you from Zion,
Light Trio:	and may you see the prosperity of Jerusalem
All Dark Trio:	all the days of your life.

All Light: Indeed, may you see your children's children,
All Dark: your children's children.
All: Behold,
All Light: children,
All Dark: children,
All Light: children are a gift,
All Dark: a gift,
All: children are a gift of the Lord.

Heaven

John 14, Revelation 21 (NASB)

All:	In my Father's house are many mansions.
Light Solo:	And I saw the holy city,
Light Duet:	new Jerusalem,
Light Trio:	coming down out of heaven from God,
All Light:	made ready as a bride adorned for her husband.
All Dark:	Behold, the tabernacle of God is among men,
Dark Trio:	and he shall dwell among them,
Dark Solo:	[Echo] He shall dwell among them?
Dark Trio:	and they shall be his peoples, and God himself shall be among them.
Light Trio:	and he shall wipe away every tear from their eyes;
Light Solo:	there shall no longer be any death;
Light Solo Two:	there shall no longer be any mourning,
Light Solo Three:	or crying,
Light Solo Four:	or pain:
All Light:	the first things have passed away.
All:	I go to prepare a place for you.

All Dark:	Behold, I am making all things new.
Dark Solo:	Come here, I shall show you the bride, the wife of the Lamb.
All:	And he carried me away in the spirit to a great and high mountain and showed me
Dark Solo:	the holy city,
All Light:	Jerusalem,
All Dark:	coming down out of heaven from God,
All:	having the glory of God.
Light Quartet:	Her brilliance was like
Light Trio:	a very costly stone,
Light Duet:	as a stone
Light Solo:	of crystal clear jasper.
Dark Solo:	It had a great and high wall
Dark Duet:	with twelve gates,
Dark Trio:	and at the gates twelve angels:
Dark Quartet:	and names were written on them,
All Dark:	which are those of the twelve tribes of the sons of Israel.
All Light:	And the material of the wall was jasper;
All:	and the city was pure gold,
Light Solo:	like clear glass,
Light Solo Two:	*[Echo]* like clear glass,
Light Solo Three:	*[Echo]* clear glass,
Light Solo Four:	*[Echo]* glass.
All Dark:	The city was pure gold,
All Light:	*[Softly]* like clear glass.
Dark Solo:	The foundation stones of the city wall were adorned with every kind of precious stone.

[The following can be spoken by either light or dark voices but should be said quickly, without any pause between the words.]

Solo:	jasper,
Solo:	sapphire,
Solo:	chalcedony,
Solo:	emerald,
Solo:	sardonyx
Solo:	sardius
Solo:	chysolite,
Solo:	beryl,
Solo:	topaz,
Solo:	chrysoprase,
Solo:	jacinth,
Solo:	amethyst,
All:	and the twelve gates were

[The same soloists should say the next lines, quickly, almost to the point of saying them simultaneously.]

Solo:	pearls;
Solo:	pearls;
Solo:	pearls;
Solo:	pearls;
Solo:	pearls;
Solo:	pearls;
Solo:	pearls;
Solo:	pearls;
Solo:	pearls;
Solo:	pearls;
Solo:	pearls;
Solo:	pearls;
All Dark:	each one of the gates
All Light:	was a single pearl.
All:	And the street of the city was pure gold,

Light Solo:	like transparent glass,
Light Solo Two:	*[Echo]* like transparent glass,
Light Solo Three:	*[Echo]* transparent glass,
Light Solo Four:	*[Echo]* glass.
Dark Solo:	And I saw no temple in it,
All Light:	for the Lord God,
All Dark:	the Almighty,
All:	and the Lamb
Dark Solo:	are its temple.
All Light:	And the city has no need of the sun
All Dark:	or of the moon,
All:	for the glory of God has illumined it,
All Light:	and its lamp is the Lamb,
Light Trio:	*[Echo]* its lamp is the Lamb.
Dark Duet:	For the glory of God,
All Light:	the glory of God,
All Dark:	the glory of God,
All:	FOR THE GLORY OF GOD HAS ILLUMINED IT,
Light Trio:	and its lamp is the Lamb.

Praise

Psalm 24 (NIV)

All Dark:	The earth is the Lord's
All Light:	the earth is the Lord's,
Dark Solo:	the earth
All:	is the Lord's,
All Dark:	and everything in it,
All:	the world,
All Light:	and all who live in it;
Light Solo:	for he founded it upon the seas
Dark Solo:	and established it upon the waters.
Light Solo:	The earth
All:	is the Lord's!

[The following lines should be spoken as one sentence.]

Light Solo One:	Who
Light Solo Two:	may
Light Solo Three:	ascend
Light Solo Four:	the hill
Light Solo Five:	of the Lord?

[The following lines should be spoken as one sentence.]

Dark Solo One:	Who
Dark Solo Two:	may
Dark Solo Three:	stand
Dark Solo Four:	in his
Dark Solo Five:	holy place?
Light Solo One:	He who has clean hands
Light Duet:	and a pure heart,
Dark Solo One:	who does not lift up his soul to an idol

Dark Duet:	or swear by what is false.
All Dark:	He will receive blessing from the Lord
All Light:	and vindication from God his Savior.
Light Duet:	Such is the generation
Light Trio:	of those who seek him,
Dark Solo Two:	those who seek him,
All:	who seek your face,
Light Solo Two:	*[Echo]* your face,
All:	O God of Jacob.
(Pause)	
All Dark:	Lift up your heads, O you gates;
All Light:	be lifted up, you ancient doors,
All:	that the King of glory may come in,
All Light:	the King of glory,
All Dark:	the King of glory,
All:	that the King of glory may come in.
Light Solo:	Who is this King of glory?
Light Duet:	Who is this King of glory?
Dark Trio:	Who is this King of glory?
All:	The Lord,
Dark Solo One:	strong and mighty,
All:	the Lord,
Light Solo One:	mighty in battle,
All:	the Lord Almighty —
All Dark:	he is the King of glory.
All Light:	Lift up your heads, O you gates;
All Dark:	lift them up, you ancient doors,
All:	that the King of glory may come in.
Dark Solo One:	Who is he, this King of glory?

All Light: The Lord Almighty —
All Dark: he is the King,
All: the King of glory.

Praise

Psalm 48, Luke 19 (NIV)

Dark Solo: Praise awaits you
All: awaits you, O God, in Zion;
Light Duet: great is the Lord,
Dark Duet: great is the Lord,
Light/Dark Quartet: and most worthy of praise,
Dark Solo: in the city of our God,
Light Solo: his holy mountain.
All: It is beautiful in its loftiness, the joy of the whole earth.
All Light: Like the utmost heights of Zaphon is Mount Zion,
All Dark: the city of the great King.
Light Solo: God is in her citadels;
Dark Solo: God is in her citadels;
All: God is in her citadels.
Light Duet: When he came near the place where the road goes down the Mount of Olives,
All Light: the whole crowd of disciples began joyfully to praise God in loud voices for all the miracles they had seen:

[The next eight lines should be said simultaneously, like a crowd shouting.]

Dark Solo One: Blessed is the King.
Light Solo One: The king who comes in the name of the Lord.
Dark Solo Two: Peace in heaven.

Light Solo Two:	Glory in the highest.
Dark Solo Three:	Blessed is the king of glory.
Light Solo Three:	Peace in the heaven to the king.
Dark Solo Four:	Glory to the king who comes from God.
Light Solo Four:	The king comes bringing peace.
Dark Solo:	As he approached Jerusalem and saw the city, he wept over it.

(Pause)

Light Solo:	Mount Zion rejoices,
Light Trio:	the villages of Judah are glad.
Light Solo One:	Walk about Zion,
Dark Solo Two:	go around her,
Light Solo Two:	count her towers,
Dark Solo Three:	consider well her ramparts,
Light Solo Three:	view her citadels,
All:	that you may tell of them to the next generation.
Dark Solo One:	For this God
Dark Trio:	is our God
All Light:	for ever and ever;
All:	he will be our guide
Light Solo:	even to the end?
All:	even to the end.

Praise

Psalm 98 (NIV)

All:	Sing to the Lord a new song,
All Light:	for he has done marvelous things.
All Dark:	His right hand, and his holy arm have worked salvation for him.
All Light:	*[Softly]* The Lord
All Dark:	*[Softly]* salvation
All Light:	*[Louder]* The Lord
All Dark:	*[Louder]* salvation
All Light:	The Lord
All:	has made his salvation known
All Dark:	and revealed his righteousness
All Light:	to the nations.
Dark Solo:	He has remembered his love
Dark Duet:	and his faithfulness to the house of Israel;
All:	All the ends of the earth have seen
All Light:	the salvation,
All Dark:	the salvation
All:	of our God.
Light Solo:	Shout for joy to the Lord, all the earth.
Dark Solo:	Burst into jubilant song with music.
Light Solo:	Shout for joy
Light Solo Two:	with jubilant song

All Light:	make music to the Lord with the harp,
Dark Solo:	with the harp,
Dark Solo Two:	*[Echo]* harp,
Light Solo:	*[Echo]* harp,
Light Solo Two:	*[Echo]* harp,
Light Solo Three:	*[Echo]* harp,
All Light:	And the sound of singing,
All Dark:	with trumpets,
Dark Solo:	and sound of the ram's horn—
All Dark:	shout for joy before the Lord, the King.
All:	Let the sea resound,
Light Trio:	and everything in it,
Dark Trio:	the world, and all who live in it.
Light Trio:	Let the rivers clap their hands,
Light/Dark Trio:	let the mountains sing together for joy;
Dark Trio:	Let them sing before the Lord,
Dark Solo:	for he comes to judge the earth.
Dark Trio:	He comes to judge the earth.
Light/Dark Trio:	He comes to judge the earth.
All:	He will judge the world in righteousness
Light Solo:	and the peoples with equity.
All Light:	Sing to the Lord a new song,
All:	for he has done marvelous things!
Dark Solo:	Shout!
Light Duet:	Shout?
All Dark:	Shout!
All:	For joy!

Praise

Psalm 115 (NASB)

All Light:	Not to us,
All:	O Lord,
All Dark:	not to us,
All:	not to us, but to thy name give glory
Light Solo:	because of thy loving kindness,
Dark Solo:	because of thy truth.
All Light:	Why should now the nations say,
All Dark:	Where, now, is their God?
All:	Our God is in the heaven;
Light Duet:	He does whatever he pleases.
Dark Solo:	Their idols are silver and gold,
Light Solo:	the work of man's hands.
Dark Duet:	They have mouths,
Light Duet:	but they cannot speak.
Light Duet Two:	They have eyes,
Dark Duet Two:	but they cannot see.
Dark Trio:	They have ears,
Light Trio:	but they cannot hear.
Light Solo:	They have noses,
Dark Solo:	but they cannot smell.
All Light:	Their hands cannot feel,
All Dark:	their feet cannot walk;
All:	They cannot make a sound with their throat.
Light Solo:	*[Softly]* those who make them
Light Duet:	will become like them,

Dark Solo: Everyone who trusts *[long pause]* in them.

[The next section should move very rapidly, with voices topping the previous speeches, one group beginning to speak before the previous group has finished, to give a sense of urgency.]

All Light: O Israel, trust in the Lord:
Dark Solo: He is their help and their shield.
All Light: Ye who fear the Lord,
All: trust in the Lord.
Dark Solo: He is their help and their shield.
All Dark: O house of Aaron, trust in the Lord.
Dark Solo: He is their help and their shield.
Light Solo: The Lord has been mindful of us.
Light Solo Two: He will bless us.
Dark Solo Two: He will bless the house of Israel.
Light Solo Three: He will bless the house of Aaron.
Light/Dark Quartet: He will bless those who fear the Lord,
Light Solo: the small
Mixed Trio: together with the great.
All: *[Turning out and speaking directly toward the audience.]* May the Lord give you increase,
All Light: you and your children.
All Dark: May you be blessed of the Lord,
All: maker of heaven and earth.
Dark Solo: He will bless those who fear the Lord.

[Pause]
Dark Duet: The heavens are the heavens of the Lord, but the earth
Light Duet: he has given to the sons of men.
Dark Solo Two: The dead do not praise the Lord,
Dark Solo Three: nor do any who go down into silence;
All: But as for us,
Light Trio: we will bless the Lord
Dark Trio: from this time forth
All Dark: and forever.
All: Praise the Lord!
All: *[Toward the audience and motioning to them to join in.]* Praise the Lord!
All: *[With the audience.]* Praise the Lord!

Prayer and Praise
Psalm 145 (KJV)

Dark Solo: I will extol thee, my God, O King;
Dark Solo Two: I will bless thy name for ever
All Dark: [Echo] and ever.
Light Solo: Every day will I bless thee;
Light Solo Two: I will praise thy name for ever
All Light: [Echo] and ever.
All Dark: Great is the Lord,
All Light: and greatly to be praised;
All: and his greatness is
[Choir pauses and looks inquiringly at each other as if searching for the right word. Finally they shrug their shoulders and continue.]
All: unsearchable.
[The following sentence should begin with the voices on one side of the choir and gradually add new voices and drop out the former voices to give the effect of a stereo being turned from one speaker to another.]
All: One generation shall praise thy works to another,
[From voices on opposite ends of the choir.]
Light Duet: And shall declare thy mighty acts.
Light Solo: [Rapidly] I will speak of the glorious honor of thy majesty,
Light Solo Two: [Rapidly, topping the previous speech] and of thy wondrous works.

Dark Solo: *[Rapidly, topping the previous speech]* And men shall speak of the might of thy terrible acts
Dark Solo Two: *[Rapidly, topping the previous speech]* and I will declare thy greatness.
All/Minus Solos: They shall abundantly utter the memory of thy great goodness
Light/Dark Quartet: and shall sing of thy righteousness.
All Dark: *[Slowly]* The Lord is gracious
All Light: *[Slowly]* and full of compassion;
Light Solo: slow to anger
Dark Solo: and of great mercy.
All: The Lord is good
[Choir pauses, looks at each other, then smiles and nods in agreement.]
All: to all:
Light Trio: and his tender mercies are over all his works.
[Tempo should gradually increase from here to the end of the selection.]
Light Solo: All thy works shall praise thee, O Lord:
Light Duet: and thy saints shall bless thee.
Light Trio: They shall speak of the glory of thy kingdom
Trio/Dark Solo: To make known to the sons of men his mighty acts
Dark/Light Sextet: and the glorious majesty of his kingdom.
All Light: Thy kingdom is an everlasting kingdom,
All: and thy dominion endureth throughout all generations.

Day Of Remembrance
Psalm 137 (KJV)

All Dark:	By the rivers of Babylon,
All Light:	there we sat down
Light Solo:	yea, we wept
Dark Solo:	when we remembered
Light Solo:	Zion.
Light Solo One:	*[The words spoken by the soloists must flow together as if the sentence were spoken by one voice.]* We
Light Solo Two:	hanged
Light Solo Three:	our
Light Solo Four:	harps
Light Solo One:	upon
Light Solo Two:	the
Light Solo Three:	willows,
All Light:	*[Softly]* the willows.
Dark Solo:	For there they that carried us away captive required of us
Light Trio:	a song;
Dark Solo Two:	and they that wasted us required of us
Light Trio:	mirth,
All Dark:	saying, Sing us one of the songs of Zion.
All Light:	How shall we sing the Lord's song in a strange land?

[Pause]

Light Solo: *[Slowly]* How shall we sing the Lord's song
Light Duet: in a strange land?
Dark Solo One: *[Softly but with great intensity.]* If I forget thee, O Jerusalem,
Dark Solo Two: if I do not remember thee,
Dark Solo Three: if I prefer not Jerusalem above my chief joy,
Dark Solo One: *[Shouting]* let my right hand forget her cunning,
Dark Solo Two: let my tongue cleave to the roof of my mouth
All Dark: if I prefer not Jerusalem above my chief joy.

[Pause]
Dark Solo Three: By the rivers of Babylon,
All Light: *[Softly, echoing]* the rivers of Babylon,
Light Solo: we wept.

Trust In God

Psalm 3 (KJV)

[The first three lines should be spoken simultaneously from separate parts of the platform. The trio will include voices one through three. The fourth speaker will join only when the script calls for quartet.]

Dark Solo: *[Simultaneously]* How are they increased that trouble me!

Dark Solo Two: *[Simultaneously]* Many are they that rise up against me.

Dark Solo Three: *[Simultaneously]* Many there be which say of my soul,

Dark Solo Four: *[From a position upstage center]* There is no help for him in God.

Dark Trio: Lord!

Dark Solo Four: There is no help for him in God.

Dark Solo: How are they increased that trouble me!

Dark Solo Two: Many are they that rise up against me.

Dark Solo Three: Many there be which say of my soul,

Dark Solo Four: there is no help for him

Dark Trio: *[Interrupting]* Lord!

Dark Solo Three: But thou, O Lord, art a shield for me;

Dark Solo Two: my glory,

Dark Solo One: and the lifter up of mine head.

Dark Solo Four: There is no help.

Dark Solo One:	I cried unto the Lord with my voice,
Dark Solo Two:	and he heard me out of his holy hill.
Dark Solo Four:	There is no . . .
Dark Solo Three:	I laid me down and slept;
Dark Duet:	I awakened;
Dark Trio:	for the Lord sustained me.
Dark Solo Four:	There is . . .
Dark Trio:	I will not be afraid of ten thousand of people, that have set themselves against me round about.
Dark Solo Four:	There . . .
Dark Solo One:	*[Simultaneously]* arise, O Lord,
Dark Solo Two:	*[Simultaneously]* arise, O my God,
Dark Solo Three:	*[Simultaneously]* save me, O my God,
Dark Solo Three:	for thou hast smitten all mine enemies upon the cheek bone;
Dark Solo Two:	thou has broken the teeth of the ungodly.
Dark Solo One:	Salvation belongeth unto the Lord:
Dark Solo Four:	*[Weakly]* There is no help.
Dark Trio:	Thy blessing is upon thy people.
Dark Quartet:	Thy blessing is upon thy people.

Spiritual Gifts

Ephesians 4, Romans 12, 1 Corinthians 12 (KJV)

Dark Solo:	Unto every one of us is given
All Dark:	grace!
Light Solo:	Unto every one of us is given
All Light:	grace!
Dark/Light Duet:	According to the measure of the gift of Christ.
All:	Grace — the gift of Christ.
Dark Duet:	When he ascended up on high,
Add Light Duet:	he led captivity captive
All:	and gave gifts unto men.
Dark Solo:	And he gave some,
Dark Solo Two:	apostles;
Dark Solo:	and some,
Dark Solo Three:	prophets;
Dark Solo:	and some,
Dark Solo Four:	evangelists;
Dark Solo:	and some,
Dark Solo Five:	pastors and teachers;
Light Trio:	for the perfecting of the saints, for the work of the ministry,
Dark Trio:	for the edifying of the body of Christ:
All:	till we all come
Light Solo:	in the unity of faith,
Dark Solo:	and of the knowledge of the Son of God,
All:	unto a perfect man,

Dark Duet:	unto the measure
Add Light Duet:	of the stature
Add Dark Duet Two:	of the fulness
All:	of Christ:
Dark Duet:	Having then gifts,
Light Duet:	differing,
Dark Duet:	differing according to the grace,
Light Duet:	the grace that is given to us,
Dark Solo:	whether prophecy,
Dark Solo Two:	let us prophesy
Light Trio:	according to the proportion of faith;
Light Solo:	or ministry,
Light Duet:	let us wait on our ministering;
Dark Solo Three:	or he that teacheth,
Light Solo Two:	on teaching;
Dark Solo Four:	or he that exhorteth,
Light Solo Three:	on exhortation;
Light Duet:	he that giveth,
Dark Duet:	let him do it with simplicity;
Dark Solo:	he that ruleth,
Dark Quartet:	with diligence;
Light Solo:	he that showeth mercy,
Light Trio:	with cheerfulness.
All:	Let love be without dissimulation.
All Dark:	Now there are diversities of gifts,
All Light:	but the same Spirit.
All Dark:	And there are differences of administrations,
All Light:	but the same Lord.
All Dark:	And there are diversities of operations,

All Light:	but it is the same God
All:	which worketh all in all.
Light Solo:	But the manifestation of the Spirit
Light/Dark Duet:	is given to every man
All:	to profit withal.
Dark Solo:	For to one is given
Light Trio:	by the Spirit
Dark Solo:	the word of wisdom;
Light Solo:	to another the word of knowledge
Dark Quartet:	by the same Spirit;
Light Duet:	to another,
Dark Duet:	faith,
Light Duet:	by the same Spirit;
Dark Solo:	to another, the gifts of healing,
Dark Quartet:	by the same Spirit;
Dark Solo Two:	to another, the working of miracles;
Light Solo:	to another, prophecy;
Dark Solo Three:	to another, discerning of spirits;
Light Solo Two:	to another, diverse kinds of tongues;
Dark Solo Four:	to another, the interpretation of tongues:
Dark Solo:	but all these worketh that one and the selfsame Spirit,
All:	that one and the selfsame Spirit,
Light/Dark Duet:	dividing to every man
Dark Solo:	as he will. But unto every one of us is given
All Light:	grace!
All Dark:	Grace!
All:	The gift of Christ.

Prayer

Isaiah 65:24, Matthew 7:9-11, Luke 22:39-49 (KJV)

All:	Ask,
All Dark:	and it shall be given you:
All Light:	it shall,
All:	it shall
Light Trio:	be given you.
All:	Seek,
All Light:	and ye shall find,
All Dark:	ye shall find.
All:	Knock,
Dark Quartet:	and it shall be opened,
All Light:	it shall be opened,
All:	it shall be opened unto you.
All Dark:	For everyone that asketh,
All Light:	receiveth; and he that seeketh,
All Dark:	findeth; and to him that knocketh,
All Light:	it shall be opened,
All:	it shall be opened.
Light Solo:	What man is there of you,
Light Duet:	who, if his son ask bread,
Light Quartet:	will he give him a stone?
Light Trio:	Or, if he ask a fish,
Light Quartet:	will he give him a serpent?
All Light:	If ye then, being evil, know how to give
Light Solo:	good gifts
Light Solo Two:	unto your children,

All Light:	how much more,
All Dark:	much more,
All:	how much more
Dark Solo:	shall your Father,
Dark Trio:	which is in heaven,
All Light:	give good things,
Light Trio:	good things,
All Dark:	good things to them that ask
All:	to them that ask him?
Dark Solo:	Before they call,
Dark Solo Two:	I will answer;
Dark Duet:	While they are yet speaking,
Dark Quartet:	I will hear.
Dark Solo:	And he came out and went, as he was wont, to the Mount of Olives;
All Dark:	and his disciples also followed him.
All Light:	And when he was at the place, he said unto them,
Dark Duet:	pray,
All Light:	pray,
All Dark:	pray,
Dark Duet:	that ye enter not into temptation.
All Light:	And he was withdrawn from them about a stone's cast and kneeled down and
Light Solo:	prayed,
Dark Duet:	Father,
Dark Quartet:	Father,
Dark Duet:	Father, if thou be willing,
Dark Quartet:	if thou be willing,
Dark Duet:	remove this cup from me; neverthless, not my will,

Dark Quartet:	not my will,
Dark Duet:	but thine,
Dark Quartet:	but thine, be done.
All Dark:	Not my will,
Dark Duet:	but thine,
All Dark:	be done.
All Light:	And there appeared an angel unto him from heaven, strengthening him.
Light Solo:	And being in agony,
Light Duet:	he prayed more earnestly;
Light Trio:	and his sweat was as it were great drops of blood,
Light Quartet:	falling down to the ground.
All Light:	And when he rose up from prayer,
All Dark:	from prayer, and was come to his disciples,
Dark Solo:	he found them sleeping,
Light Solo:	he found them sleeping,
All Light:	sleeping,
All Dark:	he found them sleeping,
Dark Solo:	sleeping for sorrow.
Dark Quartet:	Why sleep ye?
All Light:	Why sleep ye?
All:	Rise and pray,
All Light:	rise and pray,
All Dark:	pray,
All:	Pray!
All Dark:	Rise and pray,
All Light:	lest ye enter into temptation.
All:	Rise! And pray!

Salvation

Romans 5 (NASB)

Dark Solo:	Therefore having been justified
Dark Quartet:	by faith,
Light Solo:	we have peace with God,
Light Trio:	peace with God,
Dark/Light Quartet:	through our Lord Jesus Christ,
Dark Solo:	through whom also we have obtained our introduction,
Dark Quartet:	by faith,
Light Solo:	into this grace
Light Trio:	in which we stand;
All:	And we exult in hope of the glory of God.
Light Solo:	for while we were still helpless,
Dark Solo:	at the right time
All Dark:	Christ died
Dark Solo:	for the ungodly.
Dark Quartet:	For one will hardly die for a righteous man;
Light Trio:	though perhaps for the good man someone would even dare to die.
Dark Solo:	But God demonstrates his own love toward us, in that
Light Trio:	while we were yet sinners,
All Light:	Christ died for us.
All Dark:	died for us.
All:	Christ died for us!
Dark Quartet:	Much more then, having now been justified

81

Light Trio:	by his blood,
Dark Quartet:	we shall be saved
All Dark:	from the wrath of God
Dark Quartet:	through him.
Light Trio:	For, if, while we were enemies, we were reconciled to God
Dark Solo:	through the death of his Son,
Light Trio:	much more, having been reconciled,
Dark Quartet:	we shall be saved by his life.
All Light:	And not only this,
All:	but we also exult in God through our Lord Jesus Christ,
Dark Solo:	through whom we have now received
All:	THE RECONCILIATION.
Dark Solo:	Therefore, just as through one man sin entered into the world,
Light Solo:	and death through sin,
Dark Solo:	and so death spread to
All:	all men,
Dark Solo:	because all sinned —
All Light:	much more,
All Dark:	MUCH MORE,
Dark Quartet:	,those who receive the abundance of grace
Light Trio:	and the gift of righteousness
Dark Solo:	will reign in life through the One,
All:	Jesus Christ,
All Dark:	that, as sin reigned in death,
All Light:	even so, grace might reign,
Light Trio:	through righteousness,
Dark Quartet:	to eternal life
All:	through Jesus Christ our Lord.

Dark Solo: Therefore, being justified
Dark Quartet: by faith,
Light Solo: we have peace with God,
Light Trio: peace with God,
All Light: through our Lord Jesus Christ,
All: Peace with God!

Money
Luke 12:15-21 (NIV)

Light Solo:	Watch out!
Light Solo Two:	Be on your guard against all kinds of greed!
Light Duet:	A man's life does not consist
Light Solo:	does not,
Light Solo Two:	not,
Light Solo Three:	not,
Light Solo Four:	not,
All Light:	not consist
Light Duet:	in the abundance of his possessions.
Light Solo:	Watch out!
All:	And he told them this parable:
All Light:	The ground of a certain
Dark Solo:	rich man
All Light:	produced a good crop.
Dark Duet:	He thought to himself,
Dark Solo:	What shall I do? I have no place to store my crops.
Dark Trio:	This is what I'll do.
Dark Solo:	I will tear down my barns
Dark Duet:	and build bigger ones,
Dark Trio:	and there will I store all my grain and my goods.
Dark Duet:	And I'll say to myself,
Dark Solo:	You have plenty of good things laid up for many years. Take life easy; eat, drink, and be merry.

All Light:	But God said to him,
All:	You fool! This very night your life will be demanded from you.
Dark Solo:	This night?
Light Duet:	Your life.
Dark Duet:	This night?
Light Trio:	Your life.
Dark Trio:	This night?
All Light:	Your life.
All:	Then who will get what you have prepared for yourself?
All Light:	This is how it will be with anyone who stores up things
Dark Solo:	for himself
All:	but is not rich toward God
All Light:	*[Softly, almost as an echo.]* You fool!

The Armor Of God

Ephesians 6:10-17 (NIV)

All:	Stand firm!
All Dark:	After you have done everything, to stand!
Light Solo:	Finally,
Light Duet:	be strong in the Lord,
Light Trio:	and in his mighty power.
Light/Dark Quartet:	Put on the full armor of God,
Dark Solo:	so that you can take your stand,
All:	take your stand
Dark Solo:	against the devil's schemes.
Light/Dark Quartet:	For we struggle,
Dark Solo Two:	we struggle?
Light Solo:	not against flesh and blood,
Light/Dark Quartet:	but against rulers,
Light/Dark Duet:	*[Echo]* rulers,
Light/Dark Quartet:	against the authorities,
Light/Dark Duet:	*[Echo]* authorities,
Light/Dark Quartet:	against the powers,
Light/Dark Duet:	*[Echo]* powers,
Light/Dark Quartet:	against the powers of this dark world,
Light/Dark Duet:	*[Echo]* powers, dark, powers,
Light/Dark Quartet:	against the spiritual forces of evil,
Light/Dark Duet:	*[Echo]* evil,
Light/Dark Quartet:	forces of evil,
All:	in the heavenly realms.

Dark Solo:	Therefore, put on the full armor of God,
Dark Trio:	so that when the day of evil comes,
All:	you may be able to stand your ground,
Dark Solo Three:	and after you have done everything, to stand.
Light Solo:	Stand.
Light Solo Two:	Stand.
Light Solo Three:	Stand.
Dark Solo:	Stand.
Dark Solo Two:	Stand firm.
All:	Stand firm!
Dark Solo Three:	With the belt of truth buckled around your waist,
All:	the full armor of God,
Light Solo:	with the breastplate of righteousness in place,
All:	the full armor of God,
Dark Solo One:	with your feet fitted with the readiness that comes from the gospel of peace,
All:	the full armor of God.
Light Trio:	In addition to all this,
Dark Trio:	take up the shield of faith,
Light Trio:	with which you can extinguish all the flaming arrows of the evil one,
All:	the full armor of God.
Dark Solo:	take the helmet of salvation
Light/Dark Duet:	and the sword of the Spirit,
Light/Dark Quartet:	the sword of the Spirit,
All:	which is the word of God.

Light Solo:	Stand.
Dark Solo:	Stand.
Light Solo Two:	Stand.
Dark Solo Two:	Stand.
Light/Dark Duet:	The full armor of God.
All:	Stand firm!

The Occult

Isaiah 8:19-20, Acts 19:13-20, 2 Chronicles 33 (NASB)

All:	To the law and to the testimony,
All Dark:	if they do not speak according to this word,
Dark Solo:	according to this word,
Dark Trio:	This word,
All Dark:	it is because they have no dawn.
All Light:	And when they say to you,
Light Trio:	Consult the mediums
Dark Solo Two:	and the wizards
Light Trio:	who whisper
Dark Solo Two:	and mutter,
Light Trio:	who whisper
Dark Solo Two:	and mutter,
Light Trio:	who whisper
Dark Solo Two:	and mutter,
Dark Solo One:	*[Over the top of light trio and dark solo two]* Should not a people consult their God?
Light Trio:	who whisper
Dark Solo Two:	and mutter,
Dark/Light Duet:	*[Over the top]* Should not a people consult their God?
Light Trio:	who whisper
Dark Solo Two:	and mutter,

Dark/Light Quartet: Should they consult the dead on behalf of the living?
All Dark: to the law and to the testimony!
All: to the law and to the testimony!
Light Solo: Manasseh was 12 years old when he bacame king,
Dark Trio: and he made his sons pass through the fire.
Light Trio: And he practiced witchcraft,
Dark Solo: used divination,
Light Duet: practiced sorcery,
All Light: and dealt with mediums
All Dark: and spiritists.
Dark Trio: He did much evil in the sight of the Lord,
All Light: provoking him to anger.
All Dark: And they captured Manasseh with hooks,
All Light: bound him with bronze chains,
Dark Solo: and took him to Babylon.
All: TO THE LAW AND TO THE TESTIMONY!
Light Solo: But also some of the Jewish exorcists
Light Duet: attempted to name over those who had the evil spirits
Light Trio: the name of the Lord Jesus, saying
Dark Trio: I adjure you by Jesus, whom Paul preaches.
Light Trio: And seven sons of one
Dark Solo: Sceva, a Jewish priest,

Light Solo:	were doing this.
Dark Trio:	And the evil spirit answered
Dark/Light Trios:	and said unto them,
Dark Trio:	I recognize Jesus, and I know about Paul, but who are you?

[The next four speeches should begin over the top of the previous speeches so that the story is told very rapidly.]

Dark Solo:	And the man in whom was the evil spirit *[next speech begins]* leaped on them
Dark Solo Two:	and subdued both *[next speech begins]* of them
Dark Solo Three:	and overpowered *[next speech begins]* them,
Dark Solo Four:	so that they fled out of that house naked and wounded.
All Light:	And this became known to all who lived in Ephesus,
All:	and fear fell upon them all,
All Dark:	and the name of the Lord Jesus was being magnified.
Light Solo:	Many also of those who had believed kept coming,
Light Duet:	confessing and disclosing their practices.
Light Trio:	And many of those who practiced magic brought their books together
Light Quartet:	and began burning them
All:	in the sight of all;
Dark Solo:	and they counted up the price of them
All Dark:	and found it 50,000 pieces of silver.

Light Solo:	So the word of the Lord
Light/Dark Duet:	was growing mightily
Light/Dark Quartet:	and prevailing!
All Dark:	To the law and to the testimony!
All:	If they do not speak according to this word,
Light Trio:	it is because they have no dawn.
Light Solo:	*[Echo]* No dawn.

Service

Matthew 20:1-16 (NIV)

All:	The kingdom of heaven is like,
Dark Solo:	like a landowner
All Dark:	who went out early in the morning to hire men to work in his vineyard.
All Light:	He agreed to pay them a denarius for the day
All:	and sent them into his vineyard.
Dark Solo:	About the third hour he went out
Light Duet:	and saw others standing in the marketplace, doing nothing.
Dark Solo:	You also go and work in my vineyard, and I will pay you whatever is right.
All:	So they went.
Light Solo:	He went out again about the sixth hour
Light Solo Two:	and the ninth hour
Light Duet:	and found still others standing around.
Dark Solo:	Why have you been standing here all day long doing nothing?
Dark Duet:	Because no one has hired us.
Dark Solo:	You also go and work in my vineyard.

All:	When evening came, the owner of the vineyard said to his foreman,
Dark Solo:	Call the workers and pay them their wages, beginning with the last ones hired and going on to the first.
Dark Duet:	The workers who were hired about the eleventh hour came,
Dark Solo:	and each received a denarius.
Light Duet:	So when those came who were hired first,
Light Quartet:	they expected to receive more,
Light Solo:	expected to receive more,
Light Solo Two:	to receive more,
Light Solo Three:	receive more.
Dark Solo:	But each one of them also received a denarius.
All:	When they received it,

[The next six lines should be spoken simultaneously.]

Light Solo One:	they began to grumble against the landowner,
Light Solo Two:	These men who were hired last worked only one hour.
Light Solo Three:	You have made them equal to us.
Light Solo Four:	We have borne the burden of the work and the heat of the day.
Dark Solo Two:	Against the landowner they began to grumble.
Dark Solo Three:	They grumbled, they grumbled, they grumbled.

(Pause)

Dark Solo: Friend, I am not being unfair to you. Didn't you agree to work for a denarius? Or are you envious because I am generous?
All Light: So the last will be first,
All Dark: and the first will be last.
Light Solo: Last,
Dark Solo: first.
Dark Solo Two: First,
Light Solo Two: last.

Missions

**Matthew 5:13-15,
Luke 8:16-18, 11:33-36 (KJV)**

Dark Solo:	Ye are the light of the world.
All Light:	No man, when he hath lighted a candle,
Light Solo:	putteth it in a secret place,
Light Solo Two:	neither under a bushel,
Light Solo Three	or putteth it under a bed,
All Light:	but setteth it on a candlestick,
Light Solo:	setteth it on a candlestick,
Light Solo Two:	on a candlestick,
Light Solo Three:	candlestick,
All Light:	that they which come in
All Dark:	may see the light.
All:	Ye are the light of the world.
Dark Solo:	Let your light
Dark Duet:	so shine
Dark Trio:	before men,
Light Solo:	let your light
Light Duet:	so shine
Light Trio:	before men,
Dark Solo:	that they may
All Dark:	see
Dark Solo:	your good works
All Light:	and glorify
All	your Father
All Light:	which is in heaven.
All:	Ye are the light of the world.
Dark Duet:	For nothing is secret.

Light Duet: Nothing is secret?
Dark Duet: Nothing is secret, that shall not be made manifest;
Light Duet: neither anything hid,
Dark Duet: Nothing hid?
Light Duet: Neither anything hid, that shall not be known and come abroad.
Light Solo: Nothing secret?
Dark Solo: Nothing hid?
All: NOTHING!
Light Solo: Ye are the light of the world.

Missions

Luke 24:46-48; Acts 1, 8, 13, 14; Matthew 28:18-20 (NASB)

All Dark:	Thus it is written,
Dark Solo:	that the Christ should suffer
Dark Solo Two:	and rise again from the dead the third day;
Dark Solo Three:	and that repentance for forgiveness of sins should be proclaimed in his name
Dark Trio:	to all the nations — beginning from Jerusalem.
All Dark:	You are witnesses of these things.
All Light:	You are witnesses,
All Dark:	are witnesses.
All:	You are witnesses of these things.
Light Trio:	You shall receive power when the Holy Spirit has come upon you;
Dark Quartet:	and you shall be
All:	my witnesses,
Dark Quartet:	my witnesses both in Jerusalem
Light Trio:	and in all Judea and Samaria
Light/Dark Quartet:	and even to the remotest part of the earth.
All:	my witnesses.

Dark Quartet:	On that day a great persecution arose against the church in Jerusalem;
Light Trio:	and they were all scattered throughout the regions of Judea and Samaria,
Dark Solo:	except the apostles.
Light Trio:	Therefore, those who had been scattered
Dark Quartet:	went about
All:	preaching the word.
Light Solo:	And Philip went down to the city of Samaria
Add Light Duet:	and began proclaiming Christ to them.
Dark Solo:	Now, when the apostles in Jerusalem heard that Samaria had received the word of God,
Add Dark Duet:	they sent them Peter and John.
All Light:	Now there were at Antioch, in the church that was there,
All Dark:	prophets and teachers.
All Light:	And while they were ministering to the Lord and fasting,
Light Solo:	the Holy Spirit said,
Dark Trio:	Set apart for me
Dark Solo:	Barnabas
Dark Solo Two:	and Saul,
Dark Trio:	for the work to which I have called them,
All Dark:	the work to which I have called them.

All Light:	Then, when they had fasted
All Dark:	and prayed and laid their hands on them,
All:	they sent them away.
Dark Duet:	So, being sent out by
Dark/Light Quartet:	the Holy Spirit,
Dark Duet:	they went . . .
Light Trio:	and it came about, that in Iconium they entered the synagogue of the Jews together,
Dark Duet:	and spoke in such a manner,
All:	that a great multitude believed,
All Dark:	both of Jews
All Light:	and of Greeks.
Dark/Light Quartet:	Therefore, they spent a long time there,
Light Trio:	speaking boldly
Dark Duet:	boldly, with reliance upon the Lord,
Light Trio:	the Lord who was bearing witness to the word of his grace,
Dark Duet:	bearing witness to the word of his grace,
All:	Ye shall be my witnesses.
Light Trio:	And after they had preached the gospel to that city,
All Dark:	and had made many disciples,
Dark Quartet:	they returned to Lystra and to Iconium and to Antioch,
Dark Duet:	strengthening the souls of the disciples,
Light Trio:	encouraging them to continue in the faith, and saying,

Dark Duet:	through many tribulations we must enter the kingdom of God.
Dark Quartet:	And when they had appointed elders for them in every church,
Light Trio:	having prayed with fasting,
All Light:	they commended them to the Lord, in whom they had believed.
All Dark:	And when they had arrived
All:	and gathered the church together,
Dark Duet:	they began to report all things that God had done with them,
Dark Quartet:	and how he had opened a door of faith to the gentiles.
All:	And they spent a long time with the disciples.
Dark Solo:	Go, therefore,
Dark Duet:	and make disciples
All:	of all nations,
Light Solo:	baptizing them
Light Trio:	in the name of the Father and the Son and the Holy Spirit,
Dark Quartet:	teaching them
All Dark:	to observe all that I commanded you;
Dark Duet:	and lo,
All:	I am with you always,
All Light:	always,
All Dark:	ALWAYS,
All:	I am with you always,
Dark Duet:	even to the end of the age.
Dark/Light Quartet:	Ye shall be my witnesses.

www.ingramcontent.com/pod-product-compliance
Lightning Source LLC
Chambersburg PA
CBHW060847050426
42453CB00008B/867